Wise Single Parents

Raising Children in a Healthy and Nurturing Environment

Vivian Venero

Library of Congress Control Number:
2011933761

ISBN 978-0-9837566-1-3

Published by
Emerge Publishing Group, LLC
Riviera Beach, FL
www.emergepublishers.com

Vivian Venero, 2011
Wise Single Parents
Raising Children in a Healthy and Nurturing Environment
1. Autobiographical. 2. Inspirational.

Printed in the United States of America

Contents

Dedication 1

About the Author...3

About the Book..9

1 You Are Your Children's #1
Role Model - Be A Positive One 11

2 Placing Your Children First
and Maintaining a Close
Relationship with Your Children 21

3 Dating as a Single Parent 31

4 Providing a Stable and Healthy
Environment For Your Children.....................35

5 Keeping an Amicable Relationship
with Your Former Spouse and Family 43

6 Step-parenting and Blended Families..............51

7 Healing Times 63

8 Stopping the Cycle 75

Dedication

This book is dedicated to my precious daughters Lauren Grace, Isabelle Sophia and step-daughter Stephanie Danielle Venero.

I also want to express my heartfelt and deepest gratitude to Adrian Freeman, for inspiring me and asking me, "What do you want to do when you grow up?"

About the Author

As a child, I spent countless hours playing with dolls and Barbie's. I loved role playing what my life would be like being happily married with a wonderful husband and family. Everything was perfect. My baby dolls were healthy and happy. My imaginary husband was a true gentleman. He was caring, faithful, respectful, and a loving father. We had a beautiful home and spent a lot of time with our friends and our family. I would plan birthday parties for my dolls and invite everyone. I also made plans to travel all over the world, including Spain, where my grandfather was born and raised.

Family was always a priority. I grew up living with my parents, grandparents, and my older brother. I had cousins that I spent plenty of time with and my soul mate, best friend, Idelio, too. Video games and electronic games were non-existent at that time. We only had dolls, Barbie's, and little play kitchens for the girls. The boys had baseball, football, cars, trucks, airplanes, and GI Joe's. Not much time was spent watching TV. Cartoons were only viewed Saturday mornings. I grew up having to spend much of my time in my father's business, at times, sleeping in a cot to cover the midnight shift. Life seemed simple and fun. Being bored never crossed my mind. In fact, I don't recall the word being in my vocabulary back then.

Holidays were spent with the family and were very meaningful. Weekends were busy with always something to do. Taking the bus to downtown to go shopping, attending church every Sunday, the movie's, the annual youth fair, the beach in the summer time, boy scouts camping trips, ballet and guitar lessons, and attending birthday parties are just a few to mention.

And let's not forget school. I was very fortunate to attend a small private Catholic school, where today more than thirty five years later, I still keep in contact with most of my friends.

In the Hispanic culture, it is common to see boys being raised with more freedom, more support in career making decisions, while the females are expected to stay home, assist with household duties, and ultimately becoming mothers.

My life as a child was very structured and family focused. Although I was raised watching my mother being a housewife and helping my father with the business, I wanted be someone important when I grew up. My family always focused on my brother's future and career. His lifelong dream was becoming an air force fighter pilot. In my mind, I believed I could be someone with a career and have a family. However, every time I mentioned what I wanted to do, there was always an excuse from my parents. Everytime I mentioned an interest in a career, I was always given negative feedback as to why that career was not a wise one to pursue.

At the age of 15, my life unexpectedly turned upside down. My parents separated and ended their marriage after 19 years. My brother was 18 and in college. My little sister was only 4 years old. She knew there was a difference, but didn't fully understand. I was 15 and caught in the middle. With no parenting advice or divorce courses offered back in the early 80's, both my parents expressed their feelings and their plans with me. They each focused on how they could hurt each other, not realizing that the one that would get ultimately affected was me. Witnessing all the drastic changes, I quickly learned that life was not going to be easy.

However, growing up in a private Catholic school, I had built faith and knew God would guide me through my challenges and struggles. Because of the way my mother was raised as the ideal Hispanic woman and watching her struggle, I had realized that

I had to move forward and prepare myself to be an independent woman in the future.

For years, my mother, sister, and I were financially impacted by the divorce. I was forced to leave private high school after beginning my senior year. I transferred to a public school with over 2,000 students and not knowing anyone.

With the assistance of my grandfather, I was able to purchase a car. I worked at my father's business part time to pay my car expenses and college. At the age of 19, I decided I needed to be more independent and left my father's business to work at Royal Caribbean Cruises Ltd. I worked full time and attended evening classes to finish my degree in Travel Industry Management. I felt my life was finally headed in the right direction. I was working for a prestigious cruise line that was growing rapidly and successfully. I accomplished my career goals and my childhood dream of seeing the world!

Two years later, I met my ex-husband. He was recently divorced with a beautiful daughter, named Stephanie. We dated for 22 months and then married. Since he was divorced with a child and came from a broken family, I assumed we both knew what a marriage entailed. I believed we would have a loving and successful marriage as I had imagined it when I was a little girl playing with my dolls. Also, knowing what it is like being a child from a divorced couple, I knew what my responsibilities were in providing a loving and a nurturing environment to my step-daughter, Stephanie.

My marriage began with struggles. At the beginning, I thought it was just adapting to change. My ex-husband's behavior and actions were shocking and difficult for me to adjust. I realized I had committed to the wrong man and made a mistake in marrying him and thought there was no turning back. I didn't want to fail in my marriage. I wanted to give it a shot and work on making him change and be a better person. Two and ½ years later our first daughter, Lauren was born. It was an exciting and important moment for me in my life. However, I realized that for him it seemed as if it was no big deal and it was very disappointing for me to accept.

After the birth of my daughter, Lauren, my life became that reality that I had always role played as a child, with the exception my marriage. I had a stable job, a beautiful home, and a great family, yet I knew the person who I was sharing my life with was not the man I had dreamed of spending the rest of my life with. For fourteen years I struggled to have a beautiful family and live the life I had always imagined with

little success. I had two daughters and a step-daughter that I, as a woman and mother, was not giving a good example. Living in a disgruntled marriage with no solution to improve and have a quality family life, I made the decision of accepting that I had to make a change for the betterment of our lives.

Because of my struggles and challenges during my parents' divorce, I kept the mistreatment of my ex-husband a secret in fear of failure, embarrassment, and in fear of not having support from my family. My separation was the greatest change in my life not only because of my broken marriage, but because I had to give up all the years of hard work I put into building a home and family. I also knew I had a long and even more challenging road ahead of me because I was adamant of making sure I would not put my daughters through the emotional pain and challenges I personally dealt with during my parent's divorce.

Having my daughters continuing a relationship with their father, grandparents, and extended family was an important task I was willing to make as a priority. The girls have kept a close relationship with their grandparents, whom are remarkable, and which has positively impacted everyone in maintaining a good-natured and serene bond amongst the rest of the family.

About the Book

This book is about moving forward in your life. It provides tips in raising children in a nurturing, stable and healthy environment. It also provides tips in keeping an amicable relationship with your former spouse and family, regardless of your past events. Children from divorced families often lead to a variety of problems in their lives down the road, both emotionally and physically.

It is our responsibility as parents to provide a loving and stable environment for the well being of your children. It is also our duty, regardless of our marital status, to guide them through a path in becoming successful adults. This God-inspired book will help families, especially single parents, to raise their children in a healthy and nurturing environment.

There comes a time when a woman needs to stop thinking about her looks and focus her energies on raising her children. This time comes at a moment of conception. A child needs a role model, not a supermodel. ~ Astrid Alauda

1 You Are Your Children's #1 Role Model – Be a Positive One!

Skills

Children are born without social skills. They learn how to behave by example, the behaviors of those around them. Parents, siblings, family, and babysitters are the first contact they have in their lives.

Children develop their good social skills through model positive behavior. Parents must teach children how to respect other people. A child learns good manners easily when you use "please" and "thank you" as a routine in your daily lives. It is in early childhood, we as parents, must also begin boosting their self-confidence.

By building confidence and positive behaviors early, you increase their chances of them becoming

successful adults. It is the most rewarding gift you can give your child. A great mistake I see many parents make is leaving the teaching of social skills to a child's nanny, babysitter, daycare staff, and teachers. What good would it do if they spent most of their time with someone who is providing positive role modeling and then at home there is no structure, stability, and respect within their own household? As single parents, we need to be more conscious of this because most divorced children are exposed to multiple household behaviors. This often leads them to confusion by mixed signals.

Children have more need of model
than of critics. ~ Carolyn Coats

Consistency

Being consistent and setting examples are very important. Discuss with your former spouse what structure you have as routine so that he or she can have a similar structure when the children are with the other parent. It is a difficult task; however, for the best interest of the child, keeping a routine for them will bring more stability in their lives. With parents sharing parental custody, a schedule for homework, dinner, and other playtime activities, should be worked out between both parents. It should be seamless to the child which parent they are with.

No matter the age of the child, you will always be their role model. If you are continuously running late for work, have poor work attendance, you are demonstrating irresponsible behavior that will cause your child to be an irresponsible adult. This also includes dropping them off tardy in school and letting them stay home on school days because they have a little headache or stomach ache. A child with perfect attendance shows them they can be responsible at an early age and boost their self-esteem. Letting a preschooler get away with not doing their homework is setting a very bad example at a very early age.

Most importantly, make sure that you share your moral values with your children. It also opens the doors to communicating and building a better relationship with your child. It will help in talking about topics such as smoking, drinking, sex, drugs, poverty, and other challenges we all face in society today. Your child should never have to fear communicating with you any issues or challenges they may be experiencing.

Bullying is a very popular topic in school children. We must all be very aware and prepared to resolve this situation and providing them with support. Demonstrate to your children, your confidence in yourself. Talk to them about your accomplishments and where has life led you. If you have low self esteem, chances are they will end up like you. Teach your child to be independent.

Teach Your Children How to Handle Stress

Living in today's stressful society is inevitable. Some days we experience more stress than others. Learn to deal with it in a positive way. There is no need to hide stress from your children. Instead, show them how to deal with it. Children often deal with stress in school. Children who learn to cope with stress at an early age are most likely to succeed in life, readily to handle any situation and challenges that arise.

Self-Esteem

One of the most important factors when raising children is building their self-esteem. Children and adults with high self-esteem cope better with challenges and negativity. They will generally have a positive attitude if you are a great role model and nurture your own self-esteem.

What do you think about yourself in general? Do you ever put yourself down in front of your children? If you're pessimistic, express, and identify yourself as an individual who is a failure, chances are your child will mirror you and feel the same way about themselves.

Adult Behavior (Role Modeling)

Children best learn that modeling behaviors are more effective than preaching. Children learn best by watching others and mimicking their behaviors. They grow up to be a product of their own environment. Most of today's sexual abusers were victims of abuse when they were children. Spouses or men who beat and abuse women today were witnesses of their fathers beating their mothers or were victims themselves.

Strive to be a positive role model for your children. Demonstrate positive qualities to your children while providing service to others. Children are more likely to show kindness, respect, compassion when observing the same qualities in you.

Setting Up Goals at Home

As parents, our job is to prepare our children for adulthood. Setting goals for children at an early age gives them a head start in life. The most important fundamentals skills to teach children are managing personal finances, getting organized, and eating healthy. Start by setting easy, specific goals that they can achieve. Rewarding your child when they achieve a goal is very satisfying and motivates them to continue achieving other goals as well as setting higher goals for themselves. When teaching children goal setting, you're guaranteeing them a bright future. By setting up goals for your children you're also building their self-esteem higher.

Finances

Understanding and managing money efficiently is very crucial in today's society. Teaching children the value of money and personal finance can be of great impact on their responsibilities and careers they choose later in life. Assign daily chores and routines. Provide them with a weekly allowance or reward you set in your household. You don't have to use real money. You can have play money, make special coins of craft paper, or create another idea of your own to reward them.

Add value to the play money and a rewards chore chart. Once your child reaches a certain amount, you can reward them with a special treat to the movies, toys, ice cream, or other fun activities.

Show your children you can save money. Teach them how to manage and maintain a budget. Have them assist you when writing out a check to pay bills. Explain where money comes from. Teach them how to invest, save, and spend wisely.

As they get older, they can have a part-time summer job and learn to manage their own finances. Open up a savings account and a checking account in the bank. With your assistance, they can manage their own savings and spending. Most importantly, lead by example. Keep in mind you are your child's role model.

Positive Thinking

With the challenges we face in today's society, one can easily get discouraged and think negatively. Children are in tune with today's negative world. The media consistently inundates us with horrifying news, such as, murders, violence, and other crimes.

Positive thinking is very powerful. Our thoughts control our behaviors and how we react to issues. If you're generally a positive person, your child will tend to be a positive child and grow up to be a positive person. Using positive affirmations with your children is a very simple task with a significant impact. You can provide positive reinforcement at a very early stage by verbalizing affirmations.

Below are a few affirmations you can say or have your child repeat them daily:

Affirmations:

I am great.

I am beautiful.

I am a loving boy/girl.

I am good at…riding my bike, math, science.

I am a good reader.

I am a fast learner.

I am smart.

I am full of great ideas.

I am friendly.

I am kind to others and they are kind to me.

I am helpful.

I am a good listener.

I express myself clearly.

I make friends easily.

I have lots of friends who love me.

I play well with others.

I am healthy.

I am strong.

I eat healthy.

I enjoy exercising.

I take good care of my body.

Helping your child create their own affirmations empowers them to feel better about themselves, develop self-confidence, and a positive attitude. It may also help them achieve their desired goals.

2 Placing Your Children First and Maintaining a Close Relationship with Your Children

Communication

As a parent, we all want to build a great relationship with our children. In any type of relationship, communication and honesty are the most valuable elements to building a strong foundation. It is considered one of the most important parenting skills. Being honest and open as possible when answering your child's questions must be said in an age-appropriate language for them to have a clear understanding. Depending on the topic, there may be some things that are not appropriate to share with them since they are not developmentally ready.

Discussing important topics such as their academics, puberty, drugs, religious views, and more provides them with knowledge which can be beneficial to your children later in life. Having these conversations also shows your children you have an interest in their well-being and builds trust between you and your child.

Prioritize Your Children's Needs

Your children should always be placed on the top list of your priorities. After a divorce, a single parent must evaluate their responsibilities to meet the needs of the child. After a separation, the challenge becomes greater when having to provide stability, guidance, and a good home.

A divorce emotionally impacts children, which can cause them to increase the chances of lower academic grades, have insecurities, have psychological and even possibly physical issues. If the parent that the child lives with primarily does not take care of the child's needs, they may feel neglected and even think they were the cause of the divorce.

Time

Help your children to feel secure by spending quality time with them. Show them they have your love and support. Get your child involved in extracurricular activities and be involved.

Time is very valuable. Draw up a schedule that you can maintain. Find a fun and short activity you can do on a daily basis. It could be something as simple as reading together, going for a walk, or taking them to the grocery store to help you.

Plan a Yearly Family Vacation

Although single parents face a tougher challenge financially, always budget at least a short annual family vacation. It does not need to be a vacation to Europe or a fancy trip at a five star hotel. You can plan something as simple as a camping trip, school field trip, or visiting family out of state. Breaking out of the routine and doing something different gives us all a break and an opportunity to build lifetime memories.

Allow your children to plan and take vacations with their other parent, grandparents, or family members.

Integrity

Society today lacks integrity. When raising your children with good values, one of the greatest gifts you can give them is teach them about integrity. It will not only benefit them, but those who are in their lives. Encourage them to always be truthful and respectful to their peers and everyone in their lives. As a parent, be very cautious about criticizing or punishing them for saying something they may have done wrong. Communicate with them what they have done incorrectly and any resulting consequences. By having thorough conversations and not punishing them, you are building more confidence, support, and the ability for them to rely on you to always tell them the truth. If you are not a truthful individual, most likely your children will head down the same path.

Building Trusting Parent-Child Relationships

Trust is fundamental when it comes to parent-child relationships and all other types of relationships. It is especially significant building trust during the teenage years. As previously mentioned to have an open communication with your child, set your expectations, be consistent, respectful, and you will gain the trust you will need to have a successful relationship. Always keep in mind that building trust is not easy; however, it only takes one incident to lose

trust. It is more difficult to rebuild and gain the trust back.

When you tell your child you are going to do something, stick to what you say you're going to do. By not keeping promises, the child develops the habit in not believing you, therefore losing trust. Don' t go off sneaking and doing things you don't want them doing. Chances are if they catch you, they will get the impression that there is no trust between the parent and child. You will be definitely setting the wrong example. Remember, actions speak louder than words. Trust is a two-way street.

Keep your cool. Let your child feel you are receptive with any sensitive situation. This is definitely a big plus when it comes to building trust. You want your child to feel that you are approachable to discuss sensitive issues. In these type of conversations, children are usually seeking guidance. If they feel that their parent is going to blow up, yell, or flip out, chances are they will go to their peers or others who give improper guidance.

In times of challenges or crisis, be there for your child. Show them they have your support. It also feeds into building self-confidence. Trusting parents are a reassurance of comfort to a child. Trust and open communication goes hand-in-hand with relationships.

The more you and your children feel confident with each other, the greater your relationship will be.

Express and Tell Your Children You Love Them Daily

There is no rule in any book that limits how much you should tell your children you love and appreciate them.

Slip special notes in their lunch boxes, backpacks, or be as creative as you can be. With today's electronic world, send them a text message or an e-card that expresses how special they are to you.

Celebrate their accomplishments no matter how simple they are. Share the excitement with them every time they lose a tooth, or get an 'A' on a difficult test. Let your child be a child. Always find something positive to say. If they come home filthy and dirty from school, say "Looks like you had a fantastic time today", rather than throwing a fit because their clothes are dirty. Children are always looking for positive reinforcement. Not only are you building their self-esteem and confidence, but you are teaching them to think positively in their lives.

Your children need your presence more
than your presents. ~ Jesse Jackson

Play With Your Children

There are plenty of activities you can do with your children, regardless of their ages. Playing with a child provides an opportunity for the parent to understand their children's development.

You can incorporate important household duties and responsibilities as play time for your child. Gardening is one example. They can have their own set of tools to water plants. Children would get a thrill of seeing a seed in a pot grow into a beautiful plant with flowers. Washing the car is another great thing to do. It gives them the opportunity to play with water. Help prepare a meal or setting up the table for dinner is another. When children are involved with these types of duties, you are building a sense of responsibility which would be very rewarding for them as adults.

Taking them to the park, a walk after dinner, or bike riding are just a few simple and fun things to do with your children.

Assigning Chores for Children

Chores are a great benefit for both the child and the parents. It teaches children responsibility, accountability, good habits, teamwork, and family unity.

You can start assigning simple chores with a toddler. Picking up their toys, throwing dirty clothes in the hamper, or wiping spills. As they get older you can teach them how to make their beds, feed a pet, help you with laundry, and other simple chores

Help your child with their chores while making it a fun experience for them. You can make up and sing a silly song or say a joke. This is a great opportunity to have a conversation with your children. This makes them complete their duties quicker, especially for teenagers. Having everyone involved in the household to do chores creates teamwork. The sense of working together not only brings family unity, but prepares them for working together with classmates. Later in life it will help them to be team players in their employment.

Recognition is fundamental for a child. Create a reward system that doesn't involve monetary value. This can include TV time, stickers, praise, and other simple, fun activities. Don't force them to do

WISE SINGLE PARENTS
RAISING CHILDREN IN A HEALTHY AND NURTURING ENVIRONMENT 19

something they do not enjoy. Teach them how to do it so they become familiarized with that particular duty, and then assign them a chore they would preferably enjoy.

Listen to Your Children

One of the most valuable gifts you can give your child in life is as simple as listening to them no matter how little or important the matter may be. Stop what you're doing, listen, and look at them when possible. Acknowledge their statements with a simple response . It is important to pay attention to their nonverbal language. Are they upset, happy, or afraid?

Early childhood communication opens the door for a better relationship in their teenage years. Listening is a two-way street. If you want your child to listen to you, take the time to listen to them.

If your child has an issue or problem, you don't have to come up with the solution for them right away. Analyze what they've said and then take action. Let them know what your action plan is and why or how they should proceed with resolving it. Not all issues are resolved immediately. Listening is definitely the first step to resolving problems. It also helps build stronger

relationships and it demonstrates you are respecting their statement.

Listening also builds confidence and trust in your relationship with your child. Allow your child to open up to you with their feelings. You could be surprised and shocked by what they have to say.

Don't worry that children never listen to you; worry that they are always watching you. ~ Robert Fulgum

3 Dating as a Single Parent

Children's Reaction to Parent Dating

Divorce brings mixed feelings of emotions and fears to children. Adjusting to a new life after losing the bonding of family unity can be devastating and add stress to everyone's lives. Young children are often more confused after a divorce. They have different opinions and feelings on seeing their parent with someone else. Kids who come from broken families where the divorce came to them as a surprise, often find it more difficult to see their parents with new friends. They find it difficult to comprehend the changes surrounding them and having to adjust to meeting new people who have the possibility of replacing their other parent.

Single Parent Dating Choices

With today's technology, there are a multitude of choices in meeting people. Many people choose online dating websites to meet others who share the same interests, goals, and backgrounds. Making wise choices is very essential if you are dating for the purpose of finding someone to build a new relationship. Make a list of the qualities your date must possess.. Always keep in mind the decisions you make now will impact the lives of your children.

Preparing Your Child for Parent Dating

After a divorce, a child needs time to adjust to new changes in their lives. They may not be ready to accept new people who have the possibility of replacing their biological parent. If your child is showing signs of distress due to the separation or divorce, don't add stress into their lives. Allow time for adjusting to all the new changes occurring in their lives.

Back to the Single World

Mostly everyone would agree that dating can be very difficult. Dating for a single parent is definitely more challenging. Keep in mind to always prioritize your children's needs. Take time to prioritize your needs for dating. Be selective when finding dating partners that would match up with your list of qualities. With today's technology, you may find more options in finding other single parents in your same situation. Research local activities in your area where you have the possibility of meeting new people.

Intimacy for Single Parents

As adults, we all feel the need for intimacy, especially when you're in a relationship. Allow time to pass and reassure that the relationship is heading in the right direction. Do not plan home dates and sleepovers while your children are at home until you know and confirm you are in a serious relationship. Set your rules on how you will handle intimacy while dating. Whether you realize it or not, you are setting the example for your children on how to handle and relate to intimacy, dating, and commitment when they grow up.

When to Introduce a Date to Your Children

Don't introduce your children right away to anyone. If you are casually dating, don't involve your children. This may only bring more confusion and create a more unstable environment. Young children may not understand why their mom or dad has many "new friends" who don't stick around. Remember to be a good role model. Don't show your kids it is all right to spend the night if you're just casually dating. Always make the children a priority. They need reassurance they will not lose the other parent to anyone else.

When to Schedule Your Dates

Plan your dates around your child's schedule so that it won't interfere with the time you spend with them. Your children and their schedule should always be a priority. Consistency in structure and balance will help the children with maintaining normalcy in their lives. If you have other single friends with children, arrange to help each other babysitting and covering for each other if the other friend is in the same situation.

4

Providing a Stable and Healthy Environment For Your Children

Healthy Eating

Maintaining healthy weight and a balanced diet is very essential for adults and children. We live in a society today where it is very easy to make poor choices. Fast foods are commonly known for advertising gimmicks that call attention to our children, tempting them to want to try out unhealthy foods. Fast foods are full of saturated fats, sugars, salt, starches, and high calories.

Excess sugars in foods and sodas can lead to Type 2 Diabetes in children. Foods high in fats and saturated fats can lead to high cholesterol, high blood pressure, heart disease, or other serious illnesses. Child obesity is a fast growing epidemic in the United States.

One out of every three children in the United States are known to be either overweight or obese, leading them to be more prone to depression and low self-esteem.

Start by teaching your children about nutrition. Explore with them eating healthy vegetables, fruits, fish, and lean meats that contain no fat. Children should know the consequences unhealthy eating can bring them if they don't take care of themselves.

Don't forget to take your children to their annual physicals and dental cleanings twice a year. It is fundamental to keep our children in optimal health.

Exercise with Children

Children today do not get the sufficient exercise to maintain their health. Video games, computers, and other electronic gadgets have taken control over how our children spend their leisure time.

With today's economic challenges, many parents have been forced to cut back on their expenses, making it difficult to have their children involved in dance, sports, or other physical activities. However, there are numerous physical activities that do not involve spending money. Bike riding together can be fun for the family, providing the exercise needed to maintain a healthy lifestyle. Walking and swimming are other options for exercising and spending time together as a family.

Child Success Depends on Family Structure and Stability

Children who live in a stable environment with both biological parents are more likely to succeed later in life as an adult. Children who live with a single parent, as long as their environment is stable and healthy, have the capability of doing as well academically and emotionally. Families with joint custody of children can also have the potential of positively impacting their children's stability and structure. Children observing similarities of structure and stability in both families are likely to have fewer behavioral, emotional, and academic issues.

Develop a Schedule / Structure

Establishing a schedule/routine and maintaining consistency can be very challenging. However, when setting up a routine in your daily lives, everything becomes much simpler. You tend to find more leisure time as well as do more of what you most enjoy. When getting your children involved with a daily schedule, you're helping your children build the skills they need in the future to survive in today's society successfully. By maintaining consistency and repetition in managing a schedule, you and your children 's time will become effective and efficient. Develop a morning routine including getting dressed, washing face, brushing teeth, and eating breakfast, etc. Make sure to have a time frame to complete each task. This will help them develop time management skills that will be essential for later use in adulthood.

One on One Opportunities With Your Children

Another great opportunity for the family is spending quality time together. It can be a simple walk in your neighborhood or mall, an afternoon at the beach, library, or an evening at a local bookstore.

Children appreciate it when you spend time with them. Make it a positive experience so they will want to repeat the occasion often.

Involve your children when practicing your faith. Teach them what you know, how you came into believing, and why. Bible classes, even at home alone with the family can have a great positive impact on everyone. Building your child's spiritual needs also builds a solid foundation with the family.

Having more than one child can be challenging; however, it is possible to spend some quality time alone with each of them from time to time. Each child wants to be praised for their own individuality. These one-on-one occasions are the best opportunities to have special conversations, bonding, and planning for their future. Tell them how special they are. They are entitled to know what a great impact they have been in your life. As daily homework and school projects are your child's responsibilities, they need your support and assistance at home. Being involved in their school activities is vital. They need reassurance of the importance of education not only from school, but from the parent.

Identifying Your Child's Talents and Provide Support

You can be holding the key to your child's future by identifying their talents early in life. Children are born with talent. It is our responsibility as a parent to recognize their abilities as early as possible to make sure they are in a program where they will respond to their educational and emotional needs.

Set high academic goals for your child. Let them know success is possible regardless of your economic or social background. Providing positive reinforcement and continuous support will help in building their self esteem. Motivation will strengthen the child's talent.

Pay attention to your child's interests. Does your child like to draw, enjoy music, has an interest in a specific hobby or sport, or retain numbers with ease? Take the time to observe your child. Do they express themselves effortlessly? Do they have difficulty in learning? It is key to identify their needs as early in life as possible, especially with children that may have a learning disability. Each child learns differently. They may need additional reinforcement or extra help. Don't ignore this. It is beneficial to the child to identify their needs and get them in the right program.

The perfect example is Justin Bieber's mother and grandparents. For those of you who don't know his story, I encourage you to watch his movie. As Justin Bieber's song states, "Never Say Never"... You never know, you may have the next rock star living in your home.

Be Involved in School or Community Organizations

Single parents with preteens and teenage children have the advantage of getting involved in community organizations. It is a benefit to, as a family, be able to make a difference in someone else's lives, thus the reward being greater when done in family unity. There are numerous organizations and activities such as school fundraisers, events such as the Autism Speaks, Susan Komen, Juvenile Diabetes, just to name a few. Feeding the homeless through your church, volunteering in hospitals, or United Way activities are other options available for families to participate together. Depending on your community, your teenage children may be required to complete community service prior to their high school graduation. Take this as an opportunity to make a difference in your community as a family.

Psychological and Emotional Help

A divorce or the loss of a parent can be a very traumatic and stressful event in a child's life no matter what the circumstances. A child's adjustments to changes after a divorce may take up to two years or longer. With divorce come many changes to the child; the changes in moving to a different home, changing schools, and loss of a parent all together. Observe your child's behaviors during these changes. How are they coping and reacting to these changes? Observe their social interactions with the friends and classmates.

Monitor their academic records. Schedule a conference with their teacher and counselors. Advise them of the changes at home. The quicker you identify any signs of depression, emotional, or behavioral changes in a child, the faster you can seek professional assistance for them, thus providing them the opportunity for them to heal faster and cope with the changes. It is our responsibility as parents to continue raising our children in a positive, healthy, and nurturing environment, despite the circumstances our lives leads us.

Ages of experience have taught humanity that the commitment of a father and mother to love and to serve one another promotes the welfare of children and the stability of society. ~Jack Kingston

5 Keeping an Amicable Relationship with Your Former Spouse and Family

A Time to Move Forward

Ending a marriage or long term commitment is never easy. When a marriage ends, no matter the outcome, there are significant changes to the couple, the children, as well as family and friends. Whether you wanted the split or not, fears of uncertainty, disruption in your daily routine, adjustments to a new life can cause confusion and stress to everyone's lives. No matter what your reason for separation, take note of it as an experience you had to go through and learn from it. There is always a reason for everything that happens and a lesson behind it. Negative experiences can turn into greater opportunities in the future. The importance is to recognize your faults, identify where you can improve, and move forward. Keep in mind, families with children will always have to compromise when making decisions for the best interest of the children. Adults can rebuild their lives; however, the children will always have their parents to cope with.

Focus on your new desires. Share with your children your new ideas. Move forward with hope. Life is precious and it is to be enjoyed and lived with joy. Children are always inspired by their parent's positive attitude.

Effective Communication

One of the most difficult tasks after a divorce is effective communication with your former spouse. Chances are that your marriage did not work due to lack of or no communication. However, it is necessary to continue focusing on maintaining effective communication with the children. There is potential, although communication may not have worked during a marriage, that there is communication after a divorce. Bring efforts into having a simple, but effective means of clear communication with your former spouse. Good Communication reduces stress, balances emotions, displays respect, honesty, and understanding.

Despite the circumstances or transitions, it is both parents' responsibility to communicate in a manner that does not become a confrontational argument causing a negative impact on the children or others involved.

Lack of effective communication builds poor communication in your relationships with your children. There can be a misperception of emotional feelings, fear, anger, resentment, guilt, and imbalance of emotions. Communicate in a positive manner to your children. Children look to their parents for reassurance. They are always in pursuit of your unconditional love.

Keeping Grandparents and Extended Family in the Loop of Your Children

Grandparents and extended family members play an important role in children's lives. Studies have shown that children who have a close relationship with their grandparents have better social skills and less behavioral issues, specifically children who come from single-household and step-families.

"Grandparents are a positive force for all families but play a significant role in families undergoing difficulties," said lead author Shalhevet Attar-Schwartz, PhD, of The Hebrew University of Jerusalem. "They can reduce the negative influence of parents separating and be a resource for children who are going through these family changes."

Both parents should encourage communication with the other parent to help their children grow in a positive environment. For the child's best interest, both parents and other family should treat each other with respect.

Both parents need to acknowledge the children have two homes. Parents must ensure the safety and comfort while the child is staying there. Develop routines that will help your child feel secure.

Children who have relationships with other family members have a better time adjusting to changes during a divorce. Keeping these relationships intact helps the children feel secure and more stable.

Despite the consequences in a divorce, it is the parent's duty to send a clear message to their children; even though the family structure has changed, family is still important from both sides.

Respecting Your Former Spouse and Family Members

After painful disagreements, hurtful feelings, during and after a divorce, there has to come a time for closure on both sides. You can't move forward in life if you continue to find ways to harm your former spouse. Ultimately, you are only hurting your children.

Forgive your former spouse and yourself. No matter the circumstances or how bad your situation was, it is time to move on, especially when children are involved. Continuous harassment of your former spouse may inhibit you from having the new life. Negativity may be detrimental to your children as well. It may also affect the relationship your children should continue to have with their family members. Let go of negative energy that may be keeping you from moving forward. Focus on new goals and how you will maintain an amicable communication with your former spouse and family. Maintain communication with family members, especially with those you were close to during your marriage. Communication and peace with both families brings sense of security and comfort to the children.

Grandparents, cousins, aunts, uncles, will continue to be family for your children. Ensure your child maintains the same means of communication and time as they spent together prior to the divorce. Keeping peace between both families provides better opportunities to share special moments such as birthdays, graduations, weddings, and other family events. Every family member from both sides have the same equal right to cherish these special moments. The children will also appreciate and will feel content in being able to share these special moments that will turn into memories to keep for a life time.

Bad Mouthing

Avoid speaking negatively about your former spouse or former family members, specifically in the presence of your children. A great form of communication is via email or text. This keeps your conversations private. Avoid telephone conversations if you feel that it may turn into an argument. Think before you speak. Once you realize a conversation is escalating or turning the wrong way, stop immediately. Avoid children overhearing any conversations about your situation. Advise your former spouse you will resume the conversation at a later time when the anger has cooled off. It is rare to resolve an issue and come to agreement during a heated discussion. Acknowledge when you do have a positive conversation, especially if you typically find it challenging to have one. A simple reply of "thank you" or "I appreciate it" will improve on your communication, making future conversations easier to manage.

Children as Messengers

Children should not be used to send messages to your former spouse, nevertheless spying on the other parent. With the multiple means of communication and technology today, texts and emails are excellent ways to send messages, if you find it difficult to have a verbal conversation. Involving your children in relaying messages is putting them in the middle of your conflict with your former spouse. It is difficult enough for the children to adjust to changes during a divorce. By utilizing your children to relay messages, you are exposing them to witness the emotional reaction of their parent. Children may not know how to react, causing a negative impact on the relationship they have with each parent. Do not use your child as a weapon for negotiations. A common tactic often used is the restriction of visitation rights in return for child support or requests for more financial support. Children need to spend quality time with both

parents. Each parent should always encourage their children to spend time with the other parent.

6 Step-parenting and Blended Families

Setting Expectations

Adjusting to a new marriage with children is always challenging. When choosing a partner who has children, you are also accepting his/her children. Put some strategies in place to help build unity and strengthen the relationship as one family. Step-parental responsibility is a rewarding gift if you apply respect, love, understanding, and affection as you would with your own children. Raising step-children can bring not only difficulties, but also potential conflicts between you and your partner. Build a relationship that is caring, loving, with mutual respect for each other.

Make it clear to them that it is not your intention to replace their biological mother or father. You want to build a relationship separate from everyone else. Create a bond that you could be a guide or mentor. If your relationship is close enough, the step-child will feel more comfortable in confiding in you. Discuss and create parenting expectations with your partner. Over time, with a positive and loving environment, children will feel happier in a nurturing environment that you have created for them.

Children's Biological Parent

When children are faced with their parents divorce, their greatest fear is the loss of their biological parent. The fear is greater and more devastating when someone else comes into their lives replacing the absence of the other parent. It is essential to create a loving environment where the child will continue to receive stability from their family. However, as a step-parent, it is our responsibility to provide an environment where the children would feel loved, find comfort, stability, and acceptance, without the threat of them losing their biological parent. Let them know they can count on you for love and support as if they were your own child. Let them know that their biological parent is and should always be their priority.

If conflict arises between your spouse and his/her former spouse, don't take sides. Do your best to reserve your opinions or judgment in the situation. Be a safe haven for the child rather than siding with your spouse/partner. Taking sides may back-fire on you, leaving the child to distrust and alienate you as part of the family.

No matter the circumstances of your spouse's divorce or current relationship with the former spouse, always show respect in the presence of the children. The biological mother and father will always be their priority. Encourage and support the continuance of having a loving relationship with their parents.

Bonding and Creating a Positive Environment with Your Step-children

When creating a bonding relationship with your step-children or step-child, make one that will last a lifetime. It is a difficult task however, highly achievable. With proper guidance, setting realistic expectations, two families can blend together successfully.

Create open communication, mutual respect, love, guidance, and trust. Set expectations with your spouse that will be equal to all the children from both sides.

Don't expect to gain their affection overnight. This takes time, sometimes years, depending on the situation and how much emphasis you put in creating a positive relationship.

Fun times and frequent trips to amusement parks may be fun, however, you are not viewing and setting the true picture of living together. Involving the children in everyday life situations as a new family will make the adjustments much easier to adapt to.

Be careful of too many changes coming at once to the children. It may be exciting for you to start a new relationship; however, the children may not feel the same way. Second marriages have a higher successful rate for couples who decide to wait two years or more before they remarry.

Start creating a bonding relationship by identifying the child's needs. All children want to feel loved. They want to feel safe, and secure. Often children living in second marriages feel the need to be appreciated. Step-children also have a role in the family. Let them know you recognize and allow them to participate in family decisions. Create an environment of open communication with your step-children and listen to them. With the stress they have already encountered with a divorce, allowing them to express their

emotions with you can help find healing and build a stronger relationship. Remember, the key is to establish a trusting and respectful relationship.

Children adjust to changes depending on their ages and their past experiences. Younger children adjust easier to new families. Teenagers may have less involvement as they are in a stage of creating their own identities. Plan routines and rituals that involves the entire family to spend time together. Beach days, movie night at home, or other simple family time helps bring unity and harmony to a family.

Make special arrangements/space for your step-children if they do not live in your household. Children with frequent visitations must have their own space, possibly even a room of their own. The basic essentials such as toothbrushes, hairbrushes, pajamas, and extra clothing should be kept in your household. Children having to pack these basics every time they visit creates a sense that they are just visitors and not part of the family. Sleeping arrangements should also be carefully considered. Air mattresses, sleeping bags, sofa sleeping, should not even be considered. Provide them an environment where they feel as comfortable as if they were in their own home.

Spending Quality Time with Your Spouse

Newly married couples without children spend quality time building their relationship prior to starting a family. New marriages with children are much more challenging based on the responsibilities and needs of raising a family at the same time.

Focus on building a strong marital bond with your spouse by planning and spending quality time together. Children who witness love, respect, trust, stability, structure, and open communication will tend to feel more secure and tend to model the same type of behavior.

Develop a schedule where you add a night or two a week to spend time alone with your spouse. A date to the movies, a quiet dinner at home, a walk in the neighborhood, lunch during the work week are just a few to mention. Keeping open communication develops and maintains a healthy relationship. Plan one yearly weekend or week getaway alone with your spouse.

An Amicable Relationship With Your Spouse's Former Spouse

You don't have to become best friends with your spouse's former spouse; however, it is essential for the emotional health of the children to be able to amicably relate to each other. There will be birthday parties, school activities, graduations, sporting events, in which everyone will have to attend.

Regardless of the circumstances your spouse and his/her former spouse has, keep your opinions to yourself, especially when children are involved. Taking sides may backfire on you with the relationship you have with your step-children. Respecting the children's biological parent and creating an amicable relationship will put everyone at ease. Promote tension-free interactions. Being cooperative with each other creates peace, comfort, and security for the children. The children deserve and would want their entire family celebrating and sharing memorable moments together.

Allow children to form their own opinions about any family members. Never express any negative sentiments about your former spouse or other family members in the presence of any of your children.

Discipline

Step-families have a greater challenge when it comes to disciplining their children. Not everyone has the same ideas or methods when disciplining a child. Spouses in step-families must set agreeable rules that will work and apply for the entire family. Once these rules are agreed, discuss with the children as a group and set in place. Discipline is usually perceived as a negative, especially for the children when knowing someone other than their biological parent can have authority. When creating disciplinary rules, make them positive. Explaining the rules and reasons should not be of a negative concern. All you are doing is setting up the expectations in your household.

Spouses have to not only agree on the rules set, but be consistent with them. After the rules are discussed amongst everyone, each parent should consult with each of their individual children.

Let the children know that the amount of discipline they receive is based on their actions. Focus on creating a home environment complete with structure, stability, love, caring and respect, then discipline may be used as a minimum.

Step-families with shared parental custody may have greater challenges when it comes to discipline. It is the biological parents responsibility to remind the children of the rules and the consequences.

Biological Children vs. Step-children.

There is no doubt that a biological parent has unconditional love for their own child. Can a step-child also receive the same unconditional love? Sure, why not? Because a child may have had a difficult time coping with divorce or loss of a parent, it may be more challenging. However, it is possible to bond and have a loving relationship with step-children, if you try hard enough.

Earn the trust and respect of the children. Having open communication is key to any relationship. Children who find someone to talk to openly and freely tend to feel more secure around that person, thus the bond grows stronger. Often, when that bond of communication is created and is strong, the step-children may find it easier to communicate with the step-parent rather than with their own biological parent.

Treat your own children and step-children equally. Expect your spouse to do the same. Each child, whether living in the household or having joint custody, have their own uniqueness. Identify their individuality and recognize them. Make them feel appreciated, loved, and part of the family.

Encourage the Siblings to Love and Respect Each Other

The greatest challenge in step-families is the siblings (children from both sides) bonding and getting along with each other. It could be a great challenge based on the fact that it was not their decision to unite both families.

When starting a new marriage, everyone focuses on the new relationship, the wedding, a new home, often overlooking how the children feel about the changes and the new family they will have to interact with. Changes can be rewarding but also very crucial and damaging if you don't take account to see the whole picture. A marriage involving step-children requires a great deal of work. Although the spouses primarily hold the basis of the relationship and the family in a marriage, if there is anyone in the family in disagreement, it can create conflict and trouble for everyone. Take the time to know how all the children feel about your changes and your decisions. As a parent, if they are having challenges with these changes, it is your responsibility to help them cope with it and adjust to the changes positively. Applying the same love and affection as you would to your own child will pay off in having

accomplished in developing a loving relationship with your step-children.

Plan fun family events that will involve all the children to spend quality time together and grow as one family. Encourage the children to love and respect each other as if they were their biological brothers or sisters.

7 | Healing Times

The Past

Recovering from a divorce or the ending of a relationship can be very difficult. However, keep in mind that although your hurt feelings and emotions may be overwhelming, you can move forward and start a new life. With the multiple numbers of resources offered in today's society, make every effort to healing so you move forward to reestablish stability in your life.

Have you ever heard the expression "Everything happens for a reason?" No matter what the circumstances were that caused you to end a relationship or divorce, analyze everything and take it as a learning experience. A loss can be the gain of a new journey once you make the decision to move forward and make improvements in your life. These experiences can help you become a stronger and wiser person if you put emphasis on taking it as a learning opportunity rather than a failure.

With a divorce comes feelings of loss, failure, uncertainties about your future, changes in your identity, and disruption of your daily routines. Stop and think of where your life has led you and where at this point would you like to go. It is quite common in people to always bring up the past. Reminiscing about the past has good and bad advantages. When focusing on a negative experience or hurtful memory, analyze what and how it has negatively impacted you. Acknowledge and analyze your failures; use them as teaching tools to help you avoid repeating the same mistakes.

When thinking of your past, focus on the good times and your accomplishments. Always cherish the good memories as well as share them with your children. It is important for them to know that you hold good memories. Regardless of the outcome and current circumstances, there are memories to be cherished for a lifetime. Keep in mind that although you may not feel the same way about your former spouse after a divorce, both of you took part in creating your children. Never hold any type of regrets, it will only hold you back from moving forward in your life. Another simple expression to take account for if you are holding any resentment from your past: Let it go.

Remember you are your children's role model. They look up to you analyzing and repeating your same behaviors. If you want your children to be successful, focus on positive behaviors that can be passed down.

Love Yourself

Healing is important in rebuilding your life after a separation or divorce and a lengthy process as well. With divorce, many emotions such as anger, fear, failure, uncertainties can rise up to the surface. Understand that all these feelings and emotions that surface are normal. It takes time to get all these emotions under control; however, make the effort to handle all your emotions. Set your own pace where you feel comfortable but don't ignore or deny your emotions. Not taking care of yourself may lead later to depression along with other health issues.

Take time to take care of your personal needs and pamper yourself once in a while. Use this as an opportunity to rediscover yourself. A divorce may also be taken as a learning experience to make you a stronger and healthier emotional person.

Recreating stability for you and your children should be a priority. Join a support group that will offer coping skills, encouragement, and guidance.

To love yourself means you accept who you are as an individual. You have self-respect, a positive self-image, feel good about yourself, and hold high moral values. Feel you are a valuable and a worthy human being. When you recognize your worthiness, those around you will feel the same way.

Love yourself by investing in personal growth and self development. Take responsibility to nurture your mind, body, and spirit. Children who witness their parents struggling with emotional issues during a divorce, causes more harm on them and delays healing for them. Children with less emotional struggles early in life have a better chance of being successful and living a happier life as an adult.

Find ways to motivate yourself as you start your new life. Create an action plan of things that will motivate you to lead a more rewarding and positive future. Begin with the use of affirmations to help boost you. As I mentioned in an earlier chapter, provide your children with easy/age appropriate affirmations that will boost their self-esteem and self identity.

Incorporate a healthy diet that you can share with your children and an exercise program to keep you healthy and fit as part of your action plan. Going back to school is always an opportunity many can take advantage.

Focusing on self-discovery, creating stability, and a positive environment quickly after a divorce or separation, will bring you quicker healing, peace, and happiness into your life.

Building Knowledge

Invest in your personal development by gaining knowledge. With today's technology there are numerous resources you can find in the comfort of your own home via internet. Single parents now have the flexibility to earn a college degree online. Take advantage of these opportunities to find progress in your life. There is just about every answer to any question or concern you have on how to cope with divorce, raising children, obtaining ideas in finding things to do, etc... You can find networks where you can chat online and share your feelings with others that may be going through your same situation.

It is essential that you read whether online, at the library or in a bookstore. No human being can ever say they know everything they need to know about life or the history of this world. The more you apply to learning something new every day, the wiser and stronger you become. Often, I hear people say they don't have time for reading, however, they do have the time to watch a few TV shows or have time for other things. You may be surprised what picking up a book for 20 minutes daily can do and the things you can apply to your life. Look for books of interest to you and how you can apply it. School age children are required to now read a minimum of 30 minutes a day. By applying the same concept with yourself, you are modeling positive behavior that will help your child enrich and gain more knowledge themselves.

Vision Board

A vision board is a tool you can use to focus on the areas you would like to make progress in your life. This powerful tool is used to create visualization that activates the universal law of attraction and begin manifesting your dreams into reality. This board is also a good tool to use to identify what changes you want in life and to stay focused on these desires.

You can create a vision board with your children. Have them create one with their own desires. This is a good way to learn to identify their own desires. Make it a fun family activity where you all can share your dreams. These boards don't have to be a simple poster boards with cut out pictures from a magazine. Be creative enough where everyone can find a place in their own rooms and use as décor. Review online resources prior to creating your vision board to obtain specific details and ideas.

Travel

For those of you who enjoy traveling, a short or long trip always helps out with healing process. When possible, at least once in your lifetime, take that special trip alone to a place where you may have always desired or find comforting, and at peace. Take the trip as a moment to self-reflect on the challenges you are facing and where you would like to be. Traveling is also an opportunity to refresh your mind and renew yourself. Breaking away from the routine is refreshing and soothing to the mind, body, and spirit.

Take vacations with your children. If you routinely took vacations and spent time together while married, continue to do so. Vacations are considered a great source of spending quality time where you build memories to cherish for a lifetime.

Spirituality

Spirituality is a popular form of healing many are turning to post divorce. The influence spirituality brings in healing is powerful because it reminds us that the universe is greater than any of our challenges. Praying, meditation, yoga, church activities, and outdoor activities involving the appreciation of nature helps us with the process of healing and allows us to move forward and build our faith.

When focusing on spirituality, it helps us understand that forgiveness can benefit ourselves. Spirituality helps release the negative energy that holds us back from moving forward in life. Focus on creating positive energy to help you rebuild your life.

Spirituality brings balance into our lives. Involve your children in church activities and kids support groups. Children are curious to know how the world was created and evolved. Reading the bible with your children is an experience that undoubtedly brings unity, peace, love, structure, wisdom, and balance in all your lives and in your home.

Create a daily routine at home to meditate, pray, or read a verse from the bible. Establishing spiritual guidance in your home brings your children closer to divine purpose.

Look at your parenting role
as a path to greater spiritual
awareness. ~ Mimi Doe

Support Groups for Single Parenting

Support groups for single parenting may offer a variety of excellent programs. Some groups offer unique ideas that may be suitable for your specific needs. Review what is offered in your local community or church prior to joining a group.

A few things to consider when researching a suitable support group are as follows: How often does the group meet? Does the group offer workshops? Is childcare provided? Do they have activities for the children?

Starting your own support group may also come as a benefit to you as well as for the whole family. Start by making a list of people you know who are single parents, friends, acquaintances, co-workers, and family

members. Decide where you will meet and how often. Create activities for the children while the parents meet. Make a list of responsibilities for each member of the group. Create an agenda for each meet. Invite speakers, and other friends, who you would think the members would benefit from having in the meet.

Support groups provides encouragement, comfort, and healing when you share your challenges with others.

Support Your Child

With any change, separation, or divorce, children need support, love, and guidance like never before. Prior to telling your children about a separation or divorce, be absolutely certain about your decision. It is important to be straight forward with them in an appropriate age language. Often children will blame themselves for the cause of the divorce. Be ready to comfort them expressing your love and support during this time. Reassure them that, although there will be changes in the household, that they will still have both parents, extended family, and friends. Be prepared to observe and identify any changes in their behaviors. Every child reacts differently depending on their emotional state, age, and love for their parents.

Short Term and Long Term Goals

Like in the beginning of every new year, start by writing short term and long term goals. Accomplishing goals help bring stability and structure quicker into our lives. It also helps stay organized and prioritize duties. It also creates a sense of success which leads to boosting your morale. Don't forget to reward yourself on your accomplishments. Focus on creating long term goals as it compromises a major element of your own personal development. Children who are exposed to goals early in life tend to be more successful in adulthood. Set simple and achievable goals for young children. Reward them as it creates motivation and builds their self-esteem. As they get older set goals that require a little bit of a challenge. It will help them build confidence in themselves.

Too often we give children
answers to remember than
problems to solve. ~ Roger Lewin

Depression

Grief, sorrow, fears, radical changes, sense of failure, and a feeling of loneliness is always accompanied by divorce. All these feelings of emotions can easily trigger depression. If you are having difficulty in coping with your changes and it is affecting your physical well-being, don't be afraid to seek help. Children witnessing parents with depression may also affect them in a negative manner.

8 Stopping the Cycle

Cycle of Abuse

It has been proven over time that abuse is a behavioral pattern learned and repeated from childhood. A child who is repeatedly verbally and physically abused by a parent will undoubtedly repeat the same treatment and behavior in the same manner. Children who witness their parents engaging in abusive behavior with their spouses or other family members will most likely create the same pattern of behavior with their own spouses when they become adults. There are many forms of abuse. The most common are verbal, physical, emotional, and sexual.

Isolation and economic abuse also falls in the category of abuse. Isolation abuse is considered when a spouse or partner isolates you from family and friends. Economic abuse is when a spouse or partner manages the money in the household, leaving you with a small allowance or nothing at all, demanding your entire paycheck. These forms of abuse may be just one or a combination of all together. Sadly, statistics show that one out of two marriages has had an incident of domestic violence or abuse. There is no economic or age boundaries in relationships with abuse. Victims of abuse are often left with emotional scarring, low self-esteem, and feelings of humiliation and worthlessness. Children raised in this type of environment may also tend to suffer, leaving them with the same emotional scarring and learned negative behavior.

Break the Habit

Break the habit of being a victim of domestic abuse or violence. If you separated or divorced for reasons of abuse, Kudos to you! Many stay in abusive marriages because of fear. They are afraid of leaving because they feel they or their children will get hurt. Unfortunately, many don't realize that they are already emotionally scared and it is causing more harm for the children in the household. Often, due to the constant abuse in a household, the children want out as much as the victim. They are victims of abuse. Children from divorced families having experienced some form of abuse during the marriage, tend to do much better and heal quicker after a divorce, if stability, structure, and normalcy are brought into their lives.

Family Structure

As difficult as your challenges may be after a separation or divorce, reestablish your priorities to bring stability and structure quickly back into your life. This process allows you and your children to heal quicker. Remember changes bring positive opportunities despite the circumstances you may be faced with. Take this moment of change to build the family life you have always dreamed of, even if the family is incomplete. There are plenty of single parents raising children in households filled with love, peace and harmony.

Good Morals in the Household

Developing and maintaining good morals in the household is very important for your children. Setting good morals provides parents ease that their children will make the right choices during any difficult situation they may encounter. Integrity, respect, and caring for others is vital when teaching your children good morals. You can start by providing them the care, respect, and honesty they are worthy of having. Children will quickly reciprocate to you and others what is given and taught to them.

With frequent exposure to violence, sexual content, foul language, just to name a few in today's society, it is vital we monitor and limit the children's television time, music, and video games. Communicate often with your children that even though they are exposed to this type of behavior, it is not an acceptable form of good moral values. Keeping open communication regarding this matter helps the nurturing of keeping good morals in your household.

Positive Parent Role Modeling

Effective positive parent role modeling is a must if you don't want your children to follow your same paths of mistakes. Granted, we all make mistakes in our lives, however, any lessons learned can be taught to prevent others from committing the same errors, specifically our children.

Take control of your life down a positive path as quickly as possible. The sooner you reestablish structure and stability in your household, the better off you and your children will be. Reminiscing about the past and continuous struggles will keep you from moving forward. Analyze yourself if you are making the same mistakes over and over. If you identify repeating the same negative habits, acknowledge your errors and make the effort to change for the better. Children mimic adult behavior. Focus on creating a positive attitude so your child grows in becoming a successful and happy adult.

Planning Your Children's Future and Success

Planning your children's future and success is the responsibility of both parents, regardless of the marital status. The children continue to have both parents, thus the support from both parents is crucial. Whether you hold an amicable relationship or you are challenged with a non cooperative former spouse, it is vital to stay on top of supporting the children from school education, college, and extracurricular activities. The children need your support and guidance from both in order to achieve their goals and lead a successful life as an adult.

Children are like clay; each experience leaves an impression and moulds them into their adult form. ~ Adele Cornish

www.ingramcontent.com/pod-product-compliance
Lightning Source LLC
LaVergne TN
LVHW021542080426
835509LV00019B/2796